HANNAH BANANA'S ICKY, STICKY COMPOSTING JOURNEY

by Jamee-Marie Edwards   illustrated by Mariano Epelbaum

PICTURE WINDOW BOOKS
a capstone imprint

Hi, I'm Hannah. I'm a little green right now. But very soon I will be an ap-*peeling*, delicious yellow.

I can't wait to share my journey as a **ripe** banana with you. Life is going to be sweet!

Snap! It's finally happening! My friends and I have been picked from the banana plant. Did you know a banana bunch is called a hand? One banana is called a finger!

We've ended up in a fruit basket on a kitchen counter. This is like being on a swing. *Swish!*

I can just imagine all the fun I will have when the time is ripe!

From the top of the fruit basket, I have an excellent view across the kitchen. I see a bucket on the counter.

Wait a minute? Is that a banana peel? *Eek!* Cousin Anna, is that you?

At first, I thought the food scraps were just trash.

But then, I realized the scraps going in this bucket are special. They are being saved for **compost**!

Soon, they will be recycled to help gardens grow big and strong. How exciting is that?

As the days go by, all kinds of stuff gets tossed into the bucket. Eggshells, coffee grounds, and apple cores. They are known as green waste.

Some food scraps, like fish or dairy, don't go in the bucket. They will make the mixture stinky. **PEW!** They belong in the trash can.

Uh-oh! Is that a brown spot? *YIKES!* There's another one and another one. I'm feeling sort of soft and squishy too.

I get tossed into the bucket. I'm way too mushy to be eaten.

The kitchen compost bucket fills up quickly. All the food scraps and I go outside. We're headed into a bigger compost bin.

The most important part of our journey is about to begin.

The food scraps and I are layered with brown waste. Brown waste includes dry leaves, twigs, and shredded cardboard.

One green layer. Then one brown layer. This is repeated until the bin is full. It's like making a lasagna. The layers help the waste break down faster.

Day by day, everything in the bin starts **decomposing**. Decomposing means breaking down into teeny-tiny pieces over time.

The pile attracts decomposers. Red wiggler worms are munching on the apple cores and Cousin Anna. Tiny **microorganisms** you can't see are here. They eat the food scraps too.

Composting takes time. It can take months for decomposers to do their job. People can help by turning over the pile with a shovel. The mixture needs the right amount of air and water.

More creepy-crawlies show up. Millipedes, sow bugs, and pill bugs. They are giving me the heebie-jeebies!

Sometimes mushrooms start growing in the pile. That's a good thing. It means the waste is breaking down and turning into compost!

Finally, the pile of waste has turned into compost. Compost looks just like dirt.

Compost gets mixed into soil to help fruits, vegetables, and flowers grow.

What an adventure! I started out as a little green banana and ended up in a compost bin. Sure my journey was a bit icky. But now I'm making sure more plants grow. Thanks to me, fruits, veggies, and flowers will thrive.

It's totally bananas what recycling food waste can do!

GLOSSARY

compost (KOM-pohst)–a mixture of rotted leaves, vegetables, and other items that are added to soil to make it richer

decompose (dee-kuhm-POHZ)–to rot or break down; a decomposer is a small creature that feeds on dead plants and animals and turns them into soil

microorganism (mye-kro-OR-gan-iz-um)–a living thing too small to be seen without a microscope

ripe (RYPE)–ready to be picked and eaten

ABOUT THE AUTHOR

Photo Credit MaseFX

Jamee-Marie Edwards is an author, STEAM educator, and literacy advocate from New York City who is on a mission to ignite imagination and inspire children through creativity and education. Her experience in school health and health education has allowed her to connect with youth on various levels. As the founder of The Me I Need To Be Program, Jamee-Marie creates accessible platforms for learning in which she merges the Arts and Sciences to provide students with the opportunity to express themselves, build confidence, and gain essential skills. Learn more about Jamee-Marie at her website maeinspireu.com

ABOUT THE ILLUSTRATOR

Mariano Epelbaum is a character designer, illustrator, and traditional 2D animator. He has been working professionally since 1996 in various disciplines of animation and illustration, where character designs tend to be very expressive and original. Currently, Mariano works as an art director on several projects. He is always trying different styles and techniques.

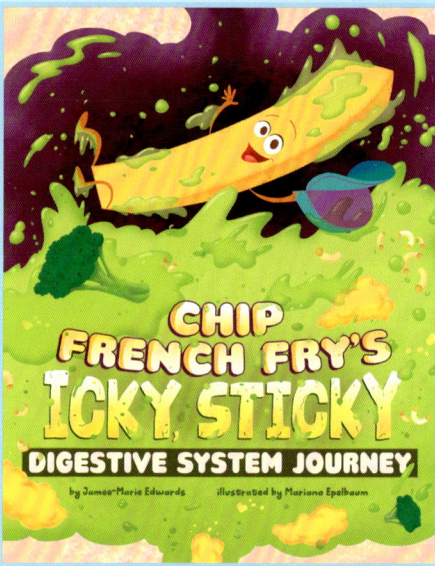

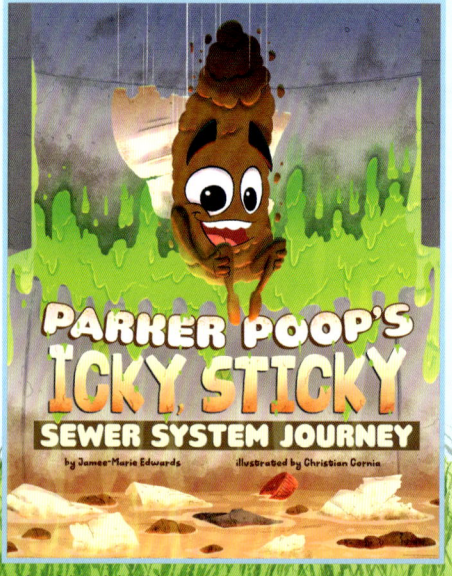

"Read more books in this series!"

Published by Picture Window Books, an imprint of Capstone
1710 Roe Crest Drive, North Mankato, Minnesota 56003
capstonepub.com

Copyright © 2026 by Capstone. All rights reserved. No part of this publication may be reproduced in whole or in part, or stored in a retrieval system, or transmitted in any form or by any means, electronic, mechanical, photocopying, recording, or otherwise, without written permission of the publisher.

Library of Congress Cataloging-in-Publication Data is available on the Library of Congress website.

ISBN: 9798875238017 (hardcover)
ISBN: 9798875237966 (paperback)
ISBN: 9798875237973 (ebook PDF)

Summary: Follow along as Hannah Banana goes from the fruit basket to the compost bucket to the compost pile and beyond. Engaging and packed with facts, this book takes readers on a step-by-step illustrated adventure to uncover the icky, sticky journey of composting.

Designer: Hilary Wacholz

Any additional websites and resources referenced in this book are not maintained, authorized, or sponsored by Capstone. All product and company names are trademarks™ or registered® trademarks of their respective holders.